John S. Huyler
The Thacher School
Ojai, Ca 93023

INFLUENCING
HORSE
BEHAVIOR

INFLUENCING HORSE BEHAVIOR
A Natural Approach to Training

Dr. Jim McCall

Illustrations by Laurie Mackenzie
Photography by Lynda McCall

1988
Alpine Publications, Inc.

First Edition

First Printing: March 1988

LIBRARY OF CONGRESS
Cataloging-in-Publication Data

McCall, Jim, 1943–
    Influencing horse behavior : A Natural Approach to Training / Jim McCall ;
illustrations by Laurie Mackenzie ; photography by Lynda McCall. — 1st Ed.
    p. cm.
    Summary: Discusses the use of behavioral principles and psychology in the
training of horses.
    ISBN: 0-931866-37-5
    1. Horses—Training. 2. Horses—Behavior. [1. Horses—Training.
2. Horses—Habits and behavior.] I. Mackenzie, Laurie, ill. II. McCall,
Lynda, ill. III. Title.
    SF287.M44 1988
    636.1'0888—dc19   88-956
                                                      CIP
                                                      AC

ISBN No. 0-9318 66-37-5

Printed in the United States of America.

iv

DEDICATION

I dedicate this book to those who have taught me about horses. First, to the professors, the horse trainers and the old cowboys who imparted some of their wisdom to me in hopes that it would be passed along to others. Second, to the two thousand plus students to whom I tried to pass on this knowledge and who challenged me to learn even more in order to answer their mind expanding questions. Third, and most importantly, to the only ones which can truly teach about horse training — the horse himself. I feel honored to have had these teachers.

ACKNOWLEDGMENTS

I wish to express my appreciation for the long hours of work that Lynda McCall, my wife, and Steve Mackenzie, my friend, spent editing this book.

Lynda took the rough ideas I presented and made them into a readable manuscript.

Steve I acknowledge for his expertise in taking that manuscript and correcting mistakes in terminology and definitions.

TABLE OF CONTENTS

Foreword

Horse trainers of all persuasions frequently feel the need to pass their knowledge on to at least one member of the next generation. Consequently they all become teachers. As such, they encounter the problem so familiar to college professors such as myself — how to select a good introductory book on the subject for outside reading. The difficulty in selection often stems from the fact that very few trainers agree on anything. So whatever book a teacher selects, chances are it won't present the material in quite the way he wants it presented. This may be one of the reasons so many educators end up writing their own books.

Naturally this leads to a large number of books on how to train horses, which causes more problems because all methods for training horses are not of equal value. It then becomes important for people to be able to discern which methods have a sound psychological basis and which do not. Just because one method works doesn't mean it is the best method for the horse. Many people treat horses in a detrimental manner but they are consistent in their treatment and eventually the horse figures out how to adapt and becomes "trained." However, in this case the horse learns what is expected of him despite what people do, not because of it.

We need to be able to select the methods which utilize good behavioral principles so that the horse can learn with the least amount of stress. In order to do that, we need to know how psychology relates to horse training. Unfortunately, many people feel that the two topics are separate. They think there is psychology on one hand and horse training on the other. They do not understand that the two are closely related. This really limits their potential as trainers, because when properly done, the training is the practical application for horse psychology.

This thinking is obvious in many young horse trainers today. For instance, the young trainers in my horse behavior and training classes think they know a lot about horse training, but what most of them actually know is the "system" of one or possibly two trainers. When I ask them to review these systems in behavioral terms and explain why one is better than others, they invariably resort to quoting philosophies of life and nature which have little to do with horses. It is obvious they have a very limited real understanding of animal behavior. They have been denied the tools necessary to compare training systems. They simply comply with what their trainer says and reiterate his philosophy on why his system is best. Hardly a good way to select training methods, but a very efficient way to maintain control of young minds.

If we are to stimulate our students to rise to the best of their abilities, we must stop controlling them and start expanding their minds. This is best done by teaching them the principles of psychology which are the tools they will need to make good decisions. This should be done relatively early in their careers. It takes time for young people to learn how to use the tools once they get them. Time and time again I get students that can spit back the definitions of behavioral terms but have no idea how to use them in the real world. That does come eventually, but only after hard work and practice. During this time period they need some good outside reading to compliment personal interaction with the teacher. This is where the separation of psychology and training in horse literature really hurts us. More books are needed on the specific use of psychology in horse training so that young trainers can have ample access to proper thinking.

This book is an excellent example of the type needed. It uses interesting stories to introduce topics and then defines specifically what is occurring behaviorally. It will make an excellent reading source for all young trainers.

Regardless of your present skill level, when you have truly mastered the principles covered in this book, you will find ways to become an even better horse trainer.

Stephen A. Mackenzie
Associate Professor
Department of Animal Science
State University of New York
Cobleskill, NY 12043

HOW TO PICK A WINNER

Today's horse needs to be a super athlete. The name of the game is competition. Gone are the days when horses were the vehicles for war, work and transportation. Within the last fifty years, the role of the horse has changed from a necessity to a leisure enjoyment. The racehorse, showhorse and the competitive riding horse have become the rule rather than the exception. The same genetic background that allowed us to ride into the twenty-first century must now produce individuals with more speed and fancier footwork.

What does it take to turn out superior athletes? It makes horse sense to compare other athletes who have been prepped to reach the pinnacle of their sport. The early Greeks believed that an athlete needed to have a superbly conditioned body and a sharp, well-disciplined mind. In the same vein, the modern Olympic athlete is not only coached in physical skills but in developing a competitive mental attitude. These human counterparts are nurtured from a very early age to maximize their inherent physical prowess. Their training programs are designed to blend the body and mind to achieve victory.

The same scenario must exist for the equine athlete. The first step in the development of a successful competitor is to analyze his behavioral make-up. The ultimate question is: What is this horse most suited to do? The answer rests in the assessment of his physical and mental skills.

Champions tend to be naturals. When searching the new generation for future competitors, coaches, teachers and trainers look for the individual with a God-given gift for the event. Even though all gifted individuals do not reach the apex in their sport, they generally reach their peak because they like it. They are programmed to excel with proper training and discipline. To judge a horse's natural athletic ability to perform in a specific event, it is necessary to have a clear, concise picture of what it takes to be that kind of athlete. You wouldn't choose a 180 pound 5-foot, 6-inch teenager to be a future figure skating champion, but you might expect him to be a good defensive lineman. It is the same with horses.

By observing natural movements, you can learn a lot about a young horse's potential.

For example, consider choosing a jumping prospect out of a group of yearlings. Begin by looking for a sure-footed horse. Placing the youngsters in a chute with a pole or cavallette on the ground would give you more information. Have someone trot the horses around the alley. Watch as they approach and go over the obstacle. The yearling that goes over with his front legs tucked up tight and his spine arched evenly is the natural. The horse that pops straight up in the air, dangling both front legs as he clears the little jump, is not a prime candidate.

If you were looking for a reining horse prospect out of the same group it would be necessary to place the young horses in a different situation. By hazing the young horses around the pen close to the fence it would be easy to see which yearling dropped down on his hocks as he sat down for the stop. The one that showed the added ability to whip around over his hocks would be the one I would drop my rope on and take home. The horse that propped on his front feet and bounced three or four times before he finally stopped would definitely be left in the pen for another event.

Visiting a farm to choose a racehorse would be an even different story. Ideally, you would observe a group of at least five to ten yearlings of the same sex in a large field where they were running and playing. The yearling that would catch my eye would consistently go to the front and, no matter what it took, refuse to let the others pass. I would be sincerely discouraged from purchasing the colt that laid back and just galloped along in a relaxed manner, not seeming to care much about running.

Other criteria exist for the pleasure horse. Watch the prospective horse move at the three major gaits: walk, trot and canter. If the yearling moves fluidly across the ground with even sweeping strides at the trot and canter, give him a solid look. Does his back seem to be motionless as he moves? Do his hocks and knees lack animation? Do his feet "clip the daisies," so to speak? If so, we might have the start of a western pleasure horse.

Having sized up your horse's natural ability, it is time to take a good look at his physical development and conformation. Today's athletic competitions are geared to the young horse. Two- and three-year-old equine athletes can bring home the money and the glory. A horse without the disposition or physical maturity to take training until three may make an excellent late performer, but the brilliance of his career is likely to be less noticeable.

Early maturity is a gift of inheritance. Proper management can make it a gold mine. Learn to recognize it when choosing future athletes. It is a trait that few champions are without.

Precociousness' perfect companion is ideal conformation. The common denominator in body structure for all breeds and in all events is straight legs and a balanced body. Yet performing in a specific event will determine the amount of emphasis placed on the ideal and the degree of tolerance accepted for individual imperfections. For example, it is imperative that our jumper prospect have powerful hindquarters, a strong top line and exceptionally sound front legs. This may lead to a minor deviation from the ideal balance, but to master tall fences the power must be located in the rear end. The front legs must then have the strength to absorb the major concussion of the landing. If the fences are going to be smaller (say three feet as in hunter events), the power in the rear end could be sacrificed as the front legs and shoulders provide more of the inertia for the smaller jumps. Size, theoretically, becomes less important as the size of the jump decreases.

Hard stops and hindquarter work are the characteristics of a reining horse. To master these maneuvers, the reining horse prospect should have power in the hindquarters with strength and soundness of hocks and rear ankles allowing him to perform with a minimum of pain. Size is related to the horse's ability to carry his rider while performing the pattern.

As we can see, stress to the body changes with the tasks asked of the horse. Of our four prospects for future competition, the pleasure horse will be stressed the least. Operating at slower speed, less trauma will be placed on the limbs and body. However, it is hard for a horse to move correctly without sound legs. To be judged on his way of going and the compatibility between horse and rider, overall conformational balance is a definite plus for this prospect.

Physical structure is often ranked number one in judging a racing prospect. Correctness of the front legs is a must. Sixty percent of the body's weight will be carried across the ground at 40 to 45 miles per hour. Add overall balance to assure an even stride that doesn't place undue stress on the body, and the basic structure of a race horse is present.

Whenever ideal conformation for an event is discussed among horsemen, the topic, invariably, turns to the exceptions: the 14-hand pony capable of jumping 6 feet; the crooked legged champion racehorse; the Thoroughbred yearling colt nobody would buy because he was too small — a colt known today as Northern Dancer, Champion Three-year-old, winner of the Derby and the Preakness and leading sire in the industry for the past two decades. There are many similar stories for all breeds in all events. Analyzing your horse's physical potential is an odds game. The odds are usually in favor of the perfect individual. Ultimately, however, conformation may tell you "the size of the man in the fight, not the size of the fight in the man." To measure the size of the fight in the man you have to look to your horse's mental disposition.

Horses show a wide variation in disposition both between and among breeds. There are individuals in all breeds which can be described as wild, timid, fearful, aggressive, playful, slow, quick, docile and more. In the four cases under consideration which characteristics would enhance the physical potential? Ideally, the jumper should be an aggressive, quick horse with a calm disposition. For the reining horse quickness is a must, but aggression would play a much important role. In the racehorse aggression and quickness are the most important. Timidity and slowness are definite undesirables. A slow, docile yearling with the correct physical attributes could make a good western pleasure horse but probably not a champion. The mark of champions, "the look of eagles,"

5

is usually seen in horses who are high ranking individuals. Their brilliance in the ring is an expression of their inherent self-confidence. To gain control of such a mind without breaking the spirit takes skill and the understanding of the basic tools of behavioral manipulation.

Horses show a wide range of dispositions both between and among breeds.

2

A CLEAR PICTURE
IS WORTH A THOUSAND CUES

 Several years ago I met a young man in his early twenties at a horse show. Being an intense and athletic sort of guy he was intrigued by the kind of horses that participated in reining events. He talked at great length to other trainers about the nature and style of a horse that would be able to run reining patterns with great precision and speed. Duly impressed, the young man decided he would enjoy riding this type of equine athlete. He set off in search of the best reining horse prospect he could find and afford.

Soon after he purchased a green-broke gray filly with a sound mind and a natural ability to do well in reining. Then the problems began. The young trainer entered the filly in a reining competition. Riding into the arena, he began to ask the filly to perform in the manner of other finished reining horses. He knew the filly was not trained to perform in a winning fashion, but he believed that if he rode her repetitively through the various reining patterns she would become increasingly more responsive and correct in the maneuvers.

This was not the case. A horse cannot comprehend a whole pattern when it does not understand each of the parts.

At first the filly tried to respond to the barrage of signals she was receiving from the rider. Before she could decipher one cue the next one was upon her. There was no relief, no reward for the effort. Consequently, the filly finally gave up trying to figure

7

out the task. She began to look for an escape. Her solution was to try and run through the bit and away from her tormentor. The young trainer snatched her head off. Driven into frustration, the young horse found no escape. Thus began the destruction of a nice filly.

Asking a horse to perform in a manner beyond its comprehension or physical abilities, or a trainer being inconsistent in his expectations about how he wishes a horse to behave, opens the doorway into learned helplessness.

This is actually a good way to push a horse into what behaviorists call learned helplessness, or laboratory neurosis. As the name implies, learned helplessness is a state in which the horse learns through several attempts that it cannot supply the proper response to a situation. It is helpless to avoid punishment. In the early stages, when learned helplessness is still a mild condition, it can be a simple case of the horse not being rewarded despite his efforts. However, if the frustration persists, and it is accompanied by punishment for incorrect responses, the horse learns that no matter what it does, it will be punished.

Asking a horse to perform in a manner beyond its comprehension or physical abilities, or a trainer being inconsistent in his expectations about how he wishes a horse to behave, opens the doorway into learned helplessness. Both of these situations lead to confusion — the source of trouble. Let's examine the case of the gray filly. She was asked to perform well beyond her skill level. Confused though she must have been, she tried her heart out to please her trainer, but nothing was good enough for him. She learned that trying produced negative results; she tried doing nothing, which also resulted in punishment. To the filly there could be only one other solution. She tried to run away from the unsolvable situation. This also resulted in severe punishment. The young horse had now tried every possible approach to the problem. All her attempts taught her the same thing. No matter what she did she would be punished. Consequently, she quit working and seemed to withdraw to prepare mentally for the inevitable punishment. Her spirit was broken.

When horses are pushed deeper and deeper into learned helplessness, many of them seem to enter this trance-like state. This seems to be a throwback behavior to their wild ancestors. Horses, as with other prey species, had to frequently experience being eaten alive by predators. Mercifully, Nature provided these species with the ability to shut down mentally when there is no escape from pain or trauma. Once in this daze, the animal seems to hear nothing, see nothing, and most important, appears to feel nothing.

The domestic horse driven into the depths of learned helplessness is in such a state. There is no escape from the pain. "To go into a sull" is the phrase used to describe this condition, but it does not seem to do justice to the emotionally distressed state which created the escape behavior. The horse is ready to die. Perhaps death would be preferred rather than the inescapable mental pain and stress. The horse becomes a vegetable. He walks, eats, grazes, but no longer gives any feedback to training.

Certain horses are born athletes, but they are made performance horses . . . Perfection is achieved in stages, and good training gets the horse from one level to the other.

The good news about learned helplessness is that it always can be avoided if you are skillful, consistent and have a clear idea about what you want to accomplish. In the example of the gray filly, the young horseman had not discussed with experienced trainers the correct manner in which to begin training a reining horse. He had not understood what performance goals are reasonable to expect at various stages of training. Certain horses are born athletes, but they are made performance horses. It is the trainer's job to

have a clear picture of how he wants each maneuver to be performed and how to get from a horse's natural ability to the performance on cue. Perfection is achieved in stages, and good training gets the horse from one level to the other.

Take for example, one of the movements found in most reining
patterns, the roll-back. To perform the roll-back, a horse in a gallop
must reverse directions by doing a 180 degree turn on his hindquarters. Although this looks like one maneuver, it is actually three
distinct moves blended into one motion. In order for a horse to
correctly execute the roll-back the basic moves should be taught
separately: the stop, the hindquarter pivot, and cantering from
a standstill on the correct lead. Each of these moves can be isolated
and practiced independently. Speed is not part of the initial training. The young prospect must first develop confidence in his ability
to execute each maneuver with precision. Only after this is accomplished should the parts be added together to produce a slow roll-
back. Speed is added last.

Don't fall into the same pit as the inexperienced trainer. Always
train with a clear picture of the successive steps necessary to
achieve the end product. A frustrated horse does not have a winning edge in the performance world. In later chapters we will dis-
cuss how to best use principles of behavioral manipulation to train
horses. But the first step is to know exactly what you want to
teach the horse every second you are in his presence.

3

EVERY ACTION HAS A REACTION

 For about 100 years, scientists have been searching for ways to identify and explain behavior. While we might describe behavior as the way an animal acts, behind the ivy covered walls of universities researchers carry this definition to the "nth" degree. Behavior is any observable or measurable movement of an organism, including external and internal movements, and glandular secretions and their combined effects.

Complicated? You bet. Yet the beauty of science to reduce complicated systems to simple terms can enable us to explain the whys, whats and hows of horse behavior. Training horses can become a lot clearer with a very basic understanding of how animal behavior, from single-celled organisms to man himself, can be manipulated,

One of the few things on which all professed behavioral experts seem to agree is that behavior is influenced by events that immediately follow. The chances that a behavior will occur again are increased if the animal is positively rewarded after the event. Behavior reoccurance is reduced if the action is met with a negative response. To stay in harmony and balance the horse will learn to make decisions that lead to his survival and well-being. Understand this simple principle, and add perception about what makes a horse a horse, and you are well on the road to becoming a horse trainer.

Horses are a unique species with specific reflexive behaviors. A reflex behavior happens involuntarily when an event causes the horse to instinctively respond in a given way. For example, a sandstorm triggers the horse's third eyelid to lower for eye protection. Heat causes horses to sweat through their skin. Reflexive responses like these happen to all members of the equine family. Yet individual horses may have their own personal fears, phobias and instinctive triggers. It is important to know what stimuli a horse may be sensitive to, and perhaps more importantly, what kind of responses may occur. By understanding such idiosyncrasies you can reduce stress and fear during training. Take, for example, throwing a saddle up on the back of a green horse. In most cases, this stimulus will trigger an emotional response, fear. How the horse handles his fear will be individual. He may run, buck, or collapse, but the response will be fear.

Many young horses are also cinchy. The first time you pull the girth they cannot stand the pressure. Bucking is a fairly uniform reflex. Having stirrups bang on a horse's sides is another stimulus which may trigger reflexive behavior. Other very sensitive horses can't handle weight on their back which does not move in balance. To say that a horse is particularly sensitive to one of these normal stimuli associated with breaking or training does not mean that the horse is going to be useless. Using very simple techniques each horse can learn to overcome his super sensitivity. The solution starts at the recognition of the horse's basic phobias and responses.

The chances that a behavior will occur again are increased if the animal is positively rewarded after the event. Behavior reoccurance is reduced if the action is met with a negative response.

Five thousand years of domestication has taught man a great deal about normal horse behavior. We know what to expect and a little bit about how to change it. A very common approach to horse training begins with the premise: Hit what comes at you. Have you heard: "If you punish a horse with pain for all the wrong efforts, and then do nothing when he makes the correct response, the absence of pain will increase the chance he will make the right move again." Or, "All horses perform at their peak, either due to pain or the suggestion of pain." Trainers who use these age old philosophies of training are molding and shaping their horse's behavior. But are they using the best method available? Let's look at some basic principles of behavior manipulation.

A key word associated with changing behavior is reinforcer—that which happens after the behavior occurs. The two types of reinforcers are those that encourage and those that discourage.

A key word associated with changing behavior is reinforcer — that which happens after the behavior occurs. The two types of reinforcers are those that encourage and those that discourage. Reinforcers that encourage a behavior are things that the trainee wants: food, water, acceptance, praise, etc. When the horse performs in the manner being sought, an encouraging reinforcer is given. This increases the odds that the behavior will occur again.

Discouraging reinforcers, on the other hand, are responses which have an aversive character such as pain or stress. It is possible for a discouraging reinforcer to be an ongoing phenomenon except when the horse performs the desired behavior. In this case, the correct response by the horse terminates the uncomfortable situation. For example, when a breeding stallion is being led to a mare, many handlers use discouraging reinforcers. Unless the horse is behaving according to the rules of the barn, he is placed under pain and stress by whipping, snatching, beating, banging and yelling. When the stallion behaves, the negative environment vanishes. This is the type of training our earlier quoted trainers are advocating. To escape the pain, the horse must make the right move. As long as the horse behaves, he avoids a negative environment.

To carry this concept one step further, when one specific behavior triggers a very uncomfortable reinforcer we have moved into the realm of punishment. Punishment is used often in training because it seems to work so well. Yet, behaviorists will tell you that the main reason it appears to work well is because it is rewarding to the punisher. When a horse bites you, punishment is certainly in order. After slugging the beast, you are immediately rewarded by the termination of his behavior. That is the positive point about punishment. Done right, it immediately eliminates the bad manners. After all, there are several things a horse can do that are hazardous to human life. Biting, kicking, striking, pawing or otherwise trying to maul humans should initiate immediate disposition of an appropriate punishment. Violence should beget violence. It is the law of nature. But, unfortunately, punishment does not shape or change undesirable behavior. It only stops it for the time being. The horseman must use that time created by the punishment to develop positive behaviors. Popping a stallion in the mouth with the leadshank button will stop his attempt to bite you.

But, the odds are ninety-nine to one he will bite again, unless this behavior can be replaced with an acceptable one.

Punishment also has some serious emotional side effects when used as the major approach to behavioral manipulation. An animal that is constantly under punishment training, may become fractious and scared. Not knowing which behavior will flare the wrath of his trainer, the horse will not take long to become afraid to make any move for fear that it will be wrong. Willingness, eagerness to learn, desire to please for human acceptance will disappear. The heart may be broken.

Encouraging reinforcement training, on the other hand, is based on rewarding the horse for his correct actions. The horse is led down a positive path to proper behavior. The animal is trained in a pleasant atmosphere where willingness and cooperation is encouraged. Training becomes learning and the horse becomes an avid student. The difficulty in using this training technique is in knowing how to reward a horse. It is easy to punish, but to reward demands some insight into the mind of the horse. How do we reward a horse? We give him something he wants; something he will always want. We target a need that can't be satisfied.

In the laboratory, experimental animals are deprived of an essential need in order to increase their desire for it. Obviously, we are not going to starve a horse to get him to perform for food or water. In the applied situation, the training pen, the reward still must be desired by the horse. Human praise and acceptance can be that reward, and a horse will work his heart out for you if you make the reward worth his effort.

As any good horseman will tell you the key to training horses is to gain the horse's respect and attention. This is also the first step to using praise as a positive encouraging reinforcer. If the human doing the praising is not respected by the horse, the praise has no value. Therefore, it cannot direct the behavior.

The second step is to offer praise in a form that the horse understands. One way a horse acknowledges praise is through touch. Suppose you are trotting a 2-year-old. You ask for a stop. His stop may not be perfect, but the colt tried and did a reasonable halt. Instead of immediately going on to the next cue, relax in the saddle and put your hand on the colt's neck immediately in front of the withers. Squeeze the neck between the thumb and fingers. This mimics reciprocal grooming — two horses that accept each other mouthing one another's neck. When reciprocal grooming occurs between two horses they are both at ease and it is a pleasurable experience. The mimic plus your relaxed attitude will make sense to the colt.

You now have the raw material of an encouraging reinforcer. Everything is a positive reference. If the horse accepts the praise and understands why the reward was given, oftentimes he will chew like a kid with a wad of bubble gum in his mouth. Chances are that the next time this colt is asked to stop, he will try to stop faster and harder.

This type of training is limited only by the horseman's ability to gain respect and convey to the horse his desires and pleasures. Unfortunately, for most of us, the ability to perform all training as perfectly as if we were in a laboratory situation is not yet within our reach. And it never can be achieved unless we learn to manipulate the behavior of a horse using positive and encouraging reinforcement.

The rewards for us are not small either. A horse trained this way will perform to the peak of his ability and understanding of your desires. Perfection will no longer be limited by your concept of how it should be done. When a horse wants to work for you, he will perform up the pinnacle of his abilities. A union of horse and horseman will exist.

Relax in the saddle and put your hand on the horse's neck in front of the withers. This mimics reciprocal grooming.

17

4
TRAINING WITH REWARDS

Developing a reward system during horse training demands an intelligent and creative mind. The advantage that nature has over us is that she has the primary reinforcers at her command. It is difficult to present a horse with food, water or sex each time a reward is necessary. Therefore, horsemen have learned to use conditioned rewards to get the job done. One of the most unique conditioned rewards that I have seen used was devised by a physics professor.

This professor, who had moved to south Texas from Ohio, had been hanging around the local rodeo arena in the evenings watching the calf ropers practice. He must have caught the bug, because, before long, he had gotten hold of an old roping horse and was trying his hand at catching calves. Everyone was a little surprised how quickly this northerner caught on. Soon he was giving the locals some fair competition. Inevitably, Dr. Physicist became dissatisfied with his horse. Getting competitive will do that to you. So, off he went to the local horse trader.

The trader must have seen the greenhorn coming. He came home with a tiny mare that was so nervous she couldn't stand her own skin. The prof was tickled. He said that the trader swore the little horse had the makings of a top roping horse if only she had the right kind of training.

For two or three months, the proud new owner spent every free moment gentling the filly and getting her in and out of the roping box. He even managed to rope a few calves on her, but every-day after tracking the first calf, the filly got so fractious and high she wouldn't do anything but stargaze and prance the rest of the night.

Finally one day I decided to offer some friendly advice to this fellow about possibly getting another horse. As I walked up to the stall I heard an unusual sound.

"Click-click. Click-click."

"That's strange," I thought to myself.

Cautiously I peeked into the stall. The filly was at the feed box eating her evening meal. The professor was talking to her in whispered tones as he brushed her. I watched, undetected, for several minutes. Again I heard the noise.

"Click-click. Click-click."

I announced my presence by asking, "What's that noise?" "Oh, it's just one of those toys that comes in a box of Cracker Jacks."

Having been to college and taken a couple of physics classes myself, I knew something about physics professors. But, this one was acting a little weirder than the norm. My curiosity got the best of me and I had to ask, "Why are you doing that?"

"I read in this book," he explained, "if you present something like a sound or light during a time when an animal is being pleasantly rewarded (like when he is eating or being groomed), that when you make the sound later the horse will associate it with the positive things. Anyway, I thought I would try it and see if it would help keep this filly from being so nervous after she tracked a calf."

Like I said, I knew physicists' brains were wired just a bit different, so I figured it best if I just went along with this book stuff and didn't mention getting another horse. "I sure hope it works for you," I said, not believing for a minute that there was a chance in Hades it would.

About a week later I was at the Wednesday night Jack-Pot roping. In rode the professor on the little bay mare. Out of the box they came. Two raps and a hooey later, the mare was still calm as a cucumber. As the prof walked toward her again I heard, "Click-click. Click-click." He climbed back in the saddle and the

20

two of them rode out of the arena. The mare was as serene as if she was standing in her stall eating oats.

In a training situation, use of conditioned rewards gives us freedom to substitute a subtle touch or sound to reward a horse after a desired behavior.

From that day to this, I've believed you can learn something about training horses from anybody — even a physics professor who reads animal behavior books. So I got myself one of those books.

The book stated that conditioned rewards will not change behavior by themselves. Bells, whistles, lights, Cracker Jack toys, money, will not cause a behavior to occur more often. Wait a minute! I know a bunch of folks reading that statement that are sure money can change behavior. Yep, you're right. But money is a conditioned reward. It is not a primary reinforcer.

It seems to work like this: food, shelter, water, love — the necessities of life — are the primary reinforcers that shape our lives as youngsters. Very early on money is paired with these basic human desires. The almighty dollar takes on power because it is paired with our basic needs and wants.

In a training situation, use of conditioned rewards gives us freedom to substitute a subtle touch or sound to reward a horse after a desired behavior. This is important during a competition when the judges don't allow time to reward the horse with a sugar lump after successfully completing a 20-foot slide during a reining pattern. If you use sugar as the reward during training, and consistently pair it with "good boy," it won't be long until the sound of good boy will be just as rewarding to the colt as the sugar lump.

At best, training with food is tricky. To always work, the horse has to always want the reward. Keeping a horse hungry, so that he will always want food, is a difficult way to achieve peak performance. However, horses always seem to want herd acceptance.

After being a herd animal for 40 million years, being accepted by the herd is a primary reinforcer. It gives the horse harmony with his environment, and he is calm, peaceful and secure. The herd is to horses as the family is to man — an evolutionary unit where one belongs. In the wild the horse will perform all manner of actions in order to stay with the herd. This herd instinct is the most powerful tool we have in training. Once understood, it can be used to manipulate the horse's behavior.

After being a herd animal for 40 million years, being accepted by the herd is a primary reinforcer. It gives the horse harmony with his environment, and he is calm, peaceful and secure.

To benefit from the power of this reinforcer, convince the horse that the two of you are a herd by giving him all the security and acceptance he expects from his equine family. This is most easily done when the horse is young. In the beginning the foal sees the herd as his mother and himself. Around 6-months of age it is easy to step into the shoes of the dam by supplying the needs of the foal. Obviously, supplying food is no problem, but providing security and acceptance may be more difficult. Once the relationship is built, however, it is easy to use a conditioned reward, like touch or sound, to trigger the acceptance reinforcer. Doing so, you reward his behavior by letting him know you are pleased to have him in your herd.

Let's move further into training to see how this technique can be used. Take a look at the young cutting horse. When a colt is asked to work hard on a cow, all impulses are strained and intense. Being in the correct position and having the perfect timing to set up a calf and hold it puts tremendous mental and physical pressure on the young horse. In the early stages of training, frequent pauses are necessary to let the colt relax and gain his composure. Placing a hand on his withers as the stop begins reminds the horse of your acceptance.

As training progresses, the need for long pauses to settle the horse disappears. As the conditioned reward triggers the serenity of herd acceptance, the cutting horse will settle down immediately after an electric exhibition simply by feeling the rider relax and by the rider's touch on his withers. The horse becomes quiet before he is asked to go back into the cattle to select another calf.

Equine behavioral modification, better known as horse training, can be built on positive training techniques. Understanding the various ways conditioned rewards can be used opens the door for trainers to invent new and better ways to achieve their goals while maintaining the horse's willing spirit.

5

THE KEY TO THE SUCCESS
OF A REWARD IS IMMEDIACY

 See if this story sounds familiar to you. You are riding about five miles from home when you find a reason to step down and leave your horse for a few minutes. When you decide to get back on, Ol' Pea Brain takes one look at you with startled surprise. As the whites of his eyes protrude from their sockets it becomes increasingly apparent that he sees you as a creature from another planet that feeds on horse blood. Of course, Ol' Pea Brain tears away, running wide open toward the safety of the barn.

Being far from home, and with a good lead on the space creature, it isn't long before your trusted mount becomes distracted from his fear by some succulent green roughage growing along the way. He stops to gorge himself. Walking up on him, you are very careful this time to announce yourself as a kind loving human who is responsible for his care and well being. You assure Ol' Pea Brain he has nothing to fear by letting you catch hold of the broken bridle reins. This time the horse is not quite as radical, but he is still suspicious of your intentions and he saunters just out of reach. By this time smoke may be bellowing from your ears as your temper waxes and your patience wanes. You realize, however, that you must remain calm and cool in order to muster another effort at catching this elusive creature. You try again. The scenario repeats itself until, finally, the home corral comes into view. On the tenth attempt at getting hold of those out-of-reach reins, you are finally successful. You have caught the critter! Good thing, because your patience is exhausted, your feet sore from walking, and most importantly, your temper long since maxed out.

What do you do to assure yourself that this incident will not be repeated? Well, if you're a perceptive, intelligent and sainted human being, the proper response is to praise Ol'Pea Brain for letting you catch him. If you are more mortal, you are more apt to beat the living daylights out of him for running away in the first place. Which way is the horse going to understand that you don't want this situation to ever happen again? Whether you reward or punish, the horse associates that activity with his most recent behavior. In this case the most recent behavior would be letting you grab hold of the reins. So do you want to punish or reward the horse? Obviously the answer is to reward or praise the horse for letting you catch him. Although, at this point, it will, understandably, take a great deal of self control.

Not every incident of immediacy is quite so contrary to human instincts. The principles of immediacy are very logical and apply to all animal behavior. The longer we wait to reinforce a behavior, the less effect the enforcer has. Conversely, the sooner after the act we reinforce, the more the behavior is modified.

Looking at another example might show the importance of this simple technique. Let's say you are going to ride a two-year-old for the first time. You climb aboard and ask the youngster to take a few steps. He takes three or four steps without jumping and exploding. Then he stops. You are real proud that this particular horse has the good sense to do what you want, and that he doesn't try to relieve himself of the burden on his back. Because you want

---

The principles of immediacy are very logical and apply to all animal behavior. The longer we wait to reinforce a behavior, the less effect the enforcer has. Conversely, the sooner after the act we reinforce, the more the behavior is modified.

---

to let him know he did well, a natural reaction would be to take a deep breath and relax, putting a hand on the colt's neck to praise him. But look at this sequence from a behavioral point of view. The horse was asked to walk. After walking a few steps, the colt stopped. You praised the colt. Although it was your intention to reward the horse for walking off easy, in reality, he has been praised for stopping. You have sent contradicting signals to this naive youngster. You asked him to go and rewarded him for stopping. If this sequence is repeated several more times, it won't be long before the youngster is sure that every time you ask him to go on, he should only go a few steps and then stop.

Unfortunately, this isn't what you want, and you may believe that the cooperative young horse you had a few minutes earlier has become balky and stubborn. What he needs is a good slap on the rump with the reins to straighten him out. Wee ha! The colt explodes from fear brought about by a misunderstanding of the minds. He tries to escape the situation by dumping the dummy on his back who doesn't seem to know giddy-up from whoa.

This sequence of events happens quite often in the breaking of a youngster. A different approach would be to ask the colt to move off by applying just a little more pressure than he can handle. The pressure could be in the form of legs, voice, seat, crop — whatever cues the young horse reads and needs as impulsion. As soon as the colt begins to move forward, remove the impulsion cues and relax. This reinforces forward movement, increasing the odds that the behavior will occur again when the impulsion cue is given.

The key to the success of reward is immediacy. The power of reinforcers to change behavior is greatly reduced as time between the action and the reward increases. This is, unfortunately, also true when the reinforcer is trying to remove undesirable behavior.

For instance, suppose you walk into the stall of an aggressive horse who tries to kick you or otherwise run you out. To fend the attack, you leave to get a stick or whip to assert your dominance. Re-entering the stall, you now proceed to beat the dickens out of the horse for previously threatening you. Confused, the horse may do one of several things. He may cower in the corner, shaking like a leaf, wondering why this maniac is beating him for no good reason. Another possible response is that the horse who didn't do anything this time might meet your confrontation head-on. Regardless of the horse's reaction to your beating, it is important to understand that he does not associate his previous undesirable behavior with your belated irate response.

Always be prepared when entering the stall of an aggressive animal who might want to fight over stall territoriality. Even unarmed, you can make an impression. Halters and leads will do as makeshift whips in a pinch. Follow an attack with a counter-attack. Yelling and charging the beast are definite signs that you are not going to submit to his domination. His behavior will not be rewarded. You may not win the round, but neither has he. Be prepared for the next time he threatens you. Immediacy and discouraging reinforcement will eliminate this unallowable behavior.

Understand that immediacy is the key to training horses with psychological principals of behavioral modification. If you are not getting your message through to your horse, take a step back and reevaluate what you are rewarding or punishing. Take a moment to look at the situation through the eyes of the horse. Is your reward paired correctly with the behavior you are trying to mold? Horses are easily conditioned to respond in a given manner. Provide the reinforcement immediately after the behavior you wish to change.

6

REINFORCEMENT PATTERNS

 At the turn of the century in Europe, a professor set out to see if he could teach arithmetic to a horse. Clever Hans, his star pupil, gained worldwide recognition as the smartest horse alive. As his reputation increased, the scientific community decided to send some of the best minds of the day to examine and test Hans' ability to do math. The professor put on a good show. He would ask the problem, the horse would paw out the answer. Hans was rewarded with a lump of sugar. The scientists were baffled.

Perhaps, they thought, the professor only asks problems to which Hans already knows the answer. So they posed the questions. Hans pawed out the answers.

They next concluded that somehow the professor must be telling the horse the answers. The panel scrutinized the professor as the problems were presented to Hans. The professor did nothing. Hans pawed out the answer. Still not convinced, the professor was asked to move to a position where Hans could not see him. A problem was given to Hans. The horse began to paw but he did not stop at the correct number. Another problem was posed. Hans missed it again. When Hans could not see the professor, he could not solve the mathematical problems.

The men of science knew they were on to something. The old professor had been communicating the correct answer to the horse. At last the tale became obvious. When Hans pawed the correct number of times, the professor's eyebrow would twitch. Reading this almost invisible facial cue, Hans had learned that if he stopped pawing a lump of sugar would be his.

A pretty remarkable feat indeed, but even more amazing if you think about the consistent performance by Hans. Trial after trial, demonstration after demonstration, there was Hans supposedly pawing out the solutions to math problems. We all should be so lucky to get our horses to behave in such a consistent manner.

What system of behavioral manipulation did the professor unwittingly use? Remember that Hans was rewarded with a lump of sugar after pawing the correct number of times. The number of times Hans had to paw to solve the problem and get the reward were randomized. For Hans, each paw might be the one which would trigger the eyebrow and get the sugar. This powerful reward schedule is known as variable ratio.

There are basically two types of reward schedules; those that reward after a number of attempts (ratio schedules), and those that reward after moments in time (interval schedules).

Over the years since, the research on this subject of reward schedules has been exhaustive and enlightening. There are basically two types of reward schedules; those that reward after a number of attempts (ratio schedules), and those that reward after moments in time (interval schedules). When training horses we are concerned primarily with ratio schedules. The use of ratio reinforcement schedules to train and maintain behavior is the secret to getting the most out of a horse.

There are two basic types of ratio schedules: variable ratio schedules and fixed ratio schedules. Several years ago, an experiment with a three-year-old Morgan mare demonstrated some important principles of these reward schedules.

The mare was placed in a twelve-foot by twelve-foot stall with solid walls and doors. A feed chute descended from the loft to a rubber bucket attached to the wall. To one side of the bucket was a block of wood hinged over a doorbell button. The first step was to teach Brilliance that flipping the wood block — which would activate the electric doorbell button — would make alfalfa pellets drop into the bucket.

In the beginning of her training whenever the mare turned in the direction of the wood block, pellets would be given. Then she had to touch the block with her nose. Then she had to flip it. Within forty-five minutes, Brilliance could get pellets upon demand. The experiment was ready to begin.

For the first three days the fixed ratio was set at two. The experimentalists wanted to determine how many times during the fifteen-minute lab session would Brilliance flip the wood block if she got pellets after each second toss. Brilliance did so twenty-four times, averaging twelve handfuls of pellets each daily session.

For the next three days the ratio was set at seven — seven flips for one reward. During the daily fifteen-minute lab sessions Brilliance worked the hinged block about eleven times each day, receiving one handful of pellets.

The final three days the ratio was set at twelve. Brilliance only flipped the lever about four times each session, and therefore, did not receive any pellets. She had passed the point at which she was willing to work for pellets.

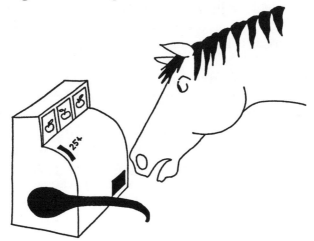

This decreasing interest in maintaining behavior which will deliver a reward is a well known phenomenon associated with fixed reward schedules. When an animal knows what it takes to get the reward he can decide whether the work is worth the effort. Obviously, Brilliance thought alfalfa pellets were worth two flips, but the cost became too great as the ratio was increased.

Her judgment also was based on the value of the reward. To measure this value, the experiment was repeated using a sugar cube as the reward. With a fixed ratio of two, the mare got twenty-three sugar lumps in fifteen minutes. At a ratio of seven, she would work for three. (The switch broke down before the final ratio schedule of twelve was tested.) Sugar was definitely worth more work.

When training horses, however, we do not want them to decide how much a reward is worth or whether they will work x number of times to get it. To avoid these problems, most horse training involves variable ratio schedules during which a reward is given after a varying number of tries. When the Morgan mare was placed on a variable ratio schedule, the pellets were presented after a randomized sequence of attempts. She would work the lever up to twenty times to get a handful of pellets.

The major advantage of this reward schedule is that horses like Brilliance and Clever Hans do not know which attempt will be rewarded. Unable to judge the relationship between the reward and the work, the horse will make more attempts to get the reward. Behavior will be maintained for longer periods between rewards.

This concept is vividly played out on the human species in casinos. Slot machines work on a variable reward schedule. It is difficult to walk away when the next quarter may trigger the next winning roll of the apples, oranges and pears. To make this system even more powerful, the slot machines tease by occasionally giving us a little taste of the reward — a handful of quarters.

Horse trainers should strive to reward their horses for proper behavior on a completely randomized variable ratio schedule. Unfortunately, many attempts at using this system are thwarted when the reward system subconsciously falls to a sequence ratio. A favorite sequence of many horsemen seems to be 1,2 then 1,2,3, or 2,3, then 2,3,4. This kind of cha-cha-cha sequence is very noticeable when a horse is being worked on a side pass. As a horse develops proficiency in the lateral crossover, many trainers unknowingly develop a pattern. They may ask the horse to make three correct lateral leg movements to the right before a pause is given. Then four more steps to the right are accomplished before another break is presented. When they change direction, six steps are taken to the left. Once completed that part of the training session is finished. If this patterned sequence is done more than a couple of times, chances are the horse will know what you are going to do before you do it.

If you have always paused at a certain point during training, but that is not always possible during competition, the horse may pause anyway. If you always change strides in the same place, the horse may start to change stride without any cue being given.

For the performance horse, learning patterns can be a definite drawback to his potential. A horse trained by sequences of movements becomes less pliable. He anticipates what is going to come next. If you have always paused at a certain point during training, but that is not possible during competition, the horse may pause anyway. If you always change strides in the same place, the horse may start to change stride without any cue being given. If a horse knows that every time he is run down the middle of the arena you are going to haul back on his mouth for a killing stop, he may start scotching or jumping in anticipation of the pain.

Horses are creatures of habit, and as trainers we can use this to our advantage. There are times early in training when it is useful for a horse to know what is expected of him, and to know that he will be rewarded for every correct response. Once the behavior is shaped, however, the possibility of winning in competition is enhanced when a horse wants to work and perform up to the limits of his own ability. To make a horse all that he can be, horsemen must understand how to effectively use reward systems. We must constantly be on guard that we do not slip into a pattern distinguishable by the horse.

7

ONE STEP AT A TIME

 As I sat on the fence watching the young rider trying to teach a green two-year-old to back for the first time, it became evident that there was a storm brewing between the horse and would-be trainer. For several minutes this young lady had been pulling back on the reins and bumping the horse's sides trying to get a back-up. The colt, in an effort to figure out what was being asked, rocked back on his hocks. When the rider failed to quit the cue, the young horse responded to what was being asked by moving a front foot backward. The rider, being impressed with her ability to train, continued on, pulling even harder on the reins and pounding the sides. Again the horse attempted to comply by moving a hind leg backward. When the pressure didn't stop, frustration began to set in. The colt quit trying to please his rider and quit moving. Fumes and sparks smoldered in the saddle and the cue to back became even more intense. In a last ditch effort the green horse tried to move forward. I guess he figured that the cue was to go forward, not backward. After all, when he had moved backward, the cue had just gotten stronger. But, the colt found he got no relief moving forward. The rider snatched the reins up and doggedly refused to let the horse move out. The colt's frustration turned to sull; he locked every joint and refused to budge no matter how much flailing and yanking was performed from his topside.

It was evident from this performance that this green rider was not familiar with the principal of successive approximation. A method of behavioral modification, successive approximation is one of the most used techniques in horse training, as well as the training of all animals, including man. In university animal behavior labs pigeons are used to demonstrate how this principal works, and to show the complex types of behavior that can be shaped. A pigeon is placed in a closed cage with a feed hopper which will deliver a food pellet upon command. To teach a pigeon to spin to the right, initially, the pigeon is rewarded with a pellet every time it makes any step to the right. Next, the pigeon has to take two steps to the right before the grain is presented. By continuing to withhold the reward until the pigeon makes more moves in the right direction, the bird can be easily trained to make beautiful 360 degree spins. The entire session from beginning to spinning pigeon takes only about ten minutes. This technique in training is so powerful that it is actually quite easy to teach a pigeon to do a reining pattern in order to obtain a food pellet.

I am of the school that believes horses are smarter and easier to train than pigeons, so it becomes a matter of figuring out how to use this type of training with horses and riders. To train a pigeon the trainer only has to be smarter than a hungry bird, but to train a horse a person has to be a little smarter than a not-so hungry horse.

A method of behavioral modification, successive approximation is one of the most used techniques in horse training, as well as the training of all animals, including man.

To produce a spinning horse, it is unreasonable to expect a green colt to perform a spin without first shaping his behavior. The approach to perfection is one of progressive improvements. The first stage is to ask the horse to move his front end laterally while

A storm is brewing. When the pressure doesn't stop, frustration begins to set in.

holding his rear end in place. This begins as a colt starts to take one or two slow fluid steps around while holding his rear legs in place. His reward is a moment of relaxation or a rub on the withers which should convey to the colt that he performed satisfactorily. Upon asking for this maneuver again, the horse should have more of an understanding and should accomplish a few steps more willingly and quicker. During the next training session, it is necessary to determine how much of the previous lesson the colt remembers. Don't just ride in and expect the horse to be willing or able to make more of the spin. Be sure the colt can perform to the level of the previous session before asking for more. After continuing

37

with this approach for three or four sessions a slow 360 degrees will begin to emerge without fear or resistance. The horse will have learned the maneuver with grace and ease, leaving speed to be added later.

To produce a spin, the first stage is to ask the horse to move his front end laterally while holding his rear end in place.

This is a very different approach from forcing the horse to perform the pivot in an all or none effort on the first attempt. Forcing a horse to perform what he doesn't understand will lead to a choppy high-headed move. Such forced training of the pivot will build fear and apprehension that can persist for months.

Successive approximation teaches a step at a time, showing the horse in small increments the task to be performed.

Successive approximation teaches a step at a time, showing the horse in small increments the task to be performed. Backing is another maneuver that lends itself well to this concept. If we return to the original scenario of the young lady and the green colt, the end result could have been different if the back was taught using successive approximation.

Here's what should have happened: as the initial backing cue was given, the rider should have used intermittent pressure on the reins to encourage the horse to back up. At the first correct movement — the rock back — pressure should have been removed and reward given. With the next backing signal, the rider should have attempted to build on the rock back and get a backward movement from any foot. Reward is important at these early stages to assure the youngster that his response to your cue is correct. Don't hammer the cue into the colt. Ask for the maneuver, reward and ride off. Weave the cue into the total work-out.

Unfortunately, in the session I watched the end result was much different. After the horse locked up, refusing to budge or even acknowledge the rider at all, I suggested that the rider tap the horse a couple of times on the poll between the ears, hoping the horse might come out of it's comatose state. The rider took me at my word, but due to her anger and frustration, popped the horse with a great deal of gusto between the ears. The horse unlocked all right, but with the same ferocity of his angry young trainer.

Lunging for the sky, the colt lost his balance and crashed to the ground. Not a pleasant experience for horse or rider, but proving again that when training horses, one small step for a horse is better than a giant step by mankind.

8

THE DISCRIMINATING HORSE

 The stallion barn at Texas A & M University sits off by itself. In the 60s it had four stalls, each with a two-acre paddock. In one of these stalls was a Quarter Horse stallion by the name of Fourable Joe. Joe was the most beautiful Quarter Horse I have ever seen, but he had a well-deserved reputation for being bad. Fourable Joe had savaged some of the best stallion men in Texas, and even at the age of 18 was not to be taken for granted.

As stallion manager, I had the job of keeping Joe in halter shape to be shown to mare owners and of handling him in the breeding shed. These tasks necessitated that Joe be caught on a daily basis. Catching Joe could be a dangerous job in itself. If I had to go into the paddock, Joe would "playfully" charge and threaten my very existence. Sometimes, however, old Joe would meet me at the gate waiting to be haltered. A rush of relief would always run over me when he came to greet me.

Soon it became obvious that Joe would meet me at the times I came to take him to the breeding shed. When I just wanted to groom him, I had to go into the paddock to get him. It puzzled me how he knew the difference. At first I assumed that the noise coming from the breeding shed foretold of the pending events. But when I changed the breeding location, he met me at the gate anyway.

I had overlooked the telltale cue. When I went to work on Joe in the stallion barn I used a nylon halter and a cotton lead. When I planned to take him out of the stud barn I always used a leather halter and a chain shank. Fourable Joe was getting his action cue from the type of halter I carried — a stimulus control.

Horses are quick to pick up on signals that indicate a certain type of behavior that is expected. This can be extremely irritating if you don't detect the signal or know how to manipulate the underlying principles.

Horses are quick to pick up on signals that indicate a certain type of behavior that is expected. This can be extremely irritating if you don't detect the signal or know how to manipulate the underlying principles.

Several years ago I was teaching horse training to two young ladies using the same horse. In the beginning, there was fierce competition between the two. Then, one of the students decided it was not necessary for both of them to work so hard on the breaking and training. She would let the other do the work. At the end of the summer, she would ride on exhibition day, demonstrating the other's accomplishments. Of course, this created a great deal of resistance from the other participant. The only response I gave her was: "It will all wash out in the end." She wheeled and fumed off.

The day of reckoning came. Each trainer was to ride his horse in a sequence of events designed to demonstrate the level of accomplishment. The hard working trainer rode first. The horse was putty in her hands. Whatever she asked, the horse tried to achieve. By the end of the session, this horse was leading the class.

The rival gloated in the wings. Soon she would be riding the same horse. Being a better rider than her conscientious partner, she was sure she could win the title of overall horse and rider team.

With worlds of confidence she stepped up on the horse and began the required exercises. From the first moment, the work began to deteriorate. The horse lacked responsiveness. Flow was nonexistent. When the rider asked for speed, her world fell apart. The superbly trained horse ran off with her. As I stepped into the arena to catch the horse, tears began to pour. She jumped down and ran out in total disgrace.

Discrimination between riders happens frequently. Your horse may work perfectly for you, but your friend cannot get him to do anything. Professional trainers tear their hair out over such situations. Hours of training produce a horse who is ready to walk into the show ring and win. Delighted with the progress of his trainer, the owner arrives at the show to ride. The trainer warms the horse up. His performance is flawless. The owner climbs into the saddle just in time to enter the class — disaster! The horse blows cue after cue. Embarrassed, the owner steams out of the arena. Hot words fly. It is not the fault of the trainer. It is not the fault of the horse. The problem is the stimulus controlling the behavior of the horse. In this situation, my best guess is that one of two signals are at work.

The show ring, itself, oftentimes, can be the stimulus which tells an old seasoned campaigner he can get away with unacceptable behavior. Since it is difficult, and even considered embarrassing, to discipline a horse in the show ring, many horses gradually realize that they can cheat.

The most obvious signal is that the horse is discriminating between the novice rider (the owner) and the trainer. Or, as in the story discussed above, he is discriminating between the hardworking novice trainer and the rival. The owner's riding skills lack the precision and expectations of the trainer. Therefore the horse will perform a different way. The solution to this problem is for the owner and trainer to work closely together until the novice rider can learn to ask for and demand the same performance.

The show ring, itself, oftentimes, can be the stimulus which tells an old seasoned campaigner he can get away with unacceptable behavior. Since it is difficult, and even considered embarrassing, to discipline a horse in the show ring, many horses gradually realize that they can cheat. Things they wouldn't dare do at home can be done without fear of reprisal. I have seen many attempts to correct this discrimination between the show ring and the training pen and most of them lack effectiveness. It does no good at all to whip the horse after the class. Immediacy is the key to correcting improper behavior. Neither will it work to give the horse the opportunity to do it again outside the ring. Even if the horse does make the mistake again, the correction out of the ring will not permanently alter the behavior. The only guaranteed cure is to reprimand the error at the time it is being made. Sacrifice the class or arrange to have mock training shows, but do not ever allow the horse to learn that different rules apply in the show ring.

We have discussed some of the ways stimulus control can disrupt training. Discrimination, however, can be a powerful training tool when used to our advantage. Going back to the Quarter Horse stallion at Texas A & M, I came to consistently use the leather halter so that the stallion would meet me at the gate. Since I was still taking him to the breeding shed on occasion, this allowed me to reward his behavior on a variable ratio schedule. He never knew which time we were going to the breeding shed, so he always met me at the gate in hopes that this time would be the time.

Many times I have used a discriminating stimulus to help curtail the behavior of rowdy studs. Since leather halters and chain shanks are always in order when handling stallions, the position of the chain can be the discriminating stimulus. Under routine handling, I like to place the chain either just through the halter or under the chin (depending on the nature of the beast). When we are going to the breeding room the chain moves to the best position for controlling a 1,000-pound breeding machine who may resist direction.

Specific tack allows a horse to expect a certain movement or action. Not only does an English saddle feel different from a

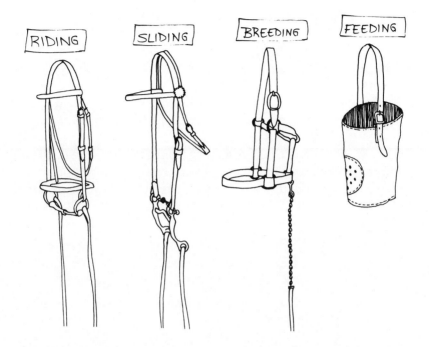

Western saddle, but the kinds of movements and maneuvers we expect while riding in each are also different.

Bits are great discriminating signals. The very structure of individual bits is designed to communicate with a horse in a specific way. Bits may apply pressure to the bars, the corners of the mouth, the tongue, the roof of the mouth, the chin, the poll or a combina-

---

Bits are great discriminating signals. The very structure of individual bits is designed to communicate with a horse in a specific way.

---

tion of points. The Racing Dee or Snaffle which uses light pressure on the bars and corner of the mouth, is often used with racehorses

45

who are asked to run into the bit. By grabbing this bit, a fast moving horse can gain forward balance and move faster into the pressure. The Snaffle is used basically in the same way for jumping horses, while English Pleasure horses may be collected on it for work on the flat. The Spanish Spade works on a completely different principle. The action of the spade uses all the possible bit pressure points. This bit allows great control for the most sensitive well-schooled mouths.

If we want different performances from the same horse, changing bits for events will help cue the horse for each performance. The more discriminating stimuli used, the better. A bit, a different saddle, a different kind of working arena, a different rider or trainer — all these signals will enhance a horse's ability to know what work is expected of him.

9
QUIT ON A GOOD NOTE

 "Tell me one thing that will make me a better trainer," the greenhorn asked. Mr. Pig Hall never looked up. I knew what he was thinking. "It sure was hard to smarten folks. If horse training was that easy, everybody would be a trainer." The silence was deafening. The old weather-beaten horse trainer glanced up from under his broad-brimmed felt hat. Begrudgingly, he mumbled, "Always quit on a good note."

His reply sounds like a good simple rule to follow. But to use this basic principle of horse training requires the finesse and feel of a master craftsman.

Consider the first question, which is bound to come up, as this would-be horse trainer tries to quit on a good note: "How long should I work my horse before looking for a quitting place?" Good things will happen throughout the work. When is enough, enough?

The answer to this inquiry is more involved than Pig Hall's one liner. First, you have to consider the attention span of the horse being ridden. Every horse has a slightly different disposition and natural intelligence. A horse with a more disciplined mind should have a longer attention span, as should the older and more mature horse. Attention also is related to subject matter and the trainer's ability to teach. A horse's desire to learn is stimulated by his teacher. Positive reinforcement coupled with the right training interval will keep a horse learning.

How long is enough? The average weanling can give you his undivided attention for about five to ten minutes. Well motivated yearlings will hang in there for ten to fifteen minutes. Two-year-olds can handle about fifteen to twenty minutes, while mature horses may be instructed for twenty to thirty minutes.

These time limits don't necessarily indicate the length of the training session. Instead the limits indicate how long to expect a horse to concentrate during the session. For example, consider a typical training plan for the young stock horse:

* Work on the stop from a walk and trot.
* After each stop, work on the back.
* Trot figure 8s, large and small.
* Work concentric circles in both directions.

At the initial stage of training, it is virtually impossible for a young horse to do each maneuver perfectly. Ask the horse to respond each time to a lighter cue, and to perform the maneuver smoother and with more confidence and quickness. This will bombard the young colt with new challenges. Boredom will be diminished by mixing up the lesson plan. In twenty minutes this youngster's mind will be used up.

At the initial stage of training, it is virtually impossible for a young horse to do each maneuver perfectly. Ask the horse to respond each time to a lighter cue, and to perform the maneuver smoother and with more confidence and quickness.

The above mentioned is the intensive training period. However, a training session is made up of two other basic parts: the warm-up and the warm-down. Before this horse works on the lessons of the day, he should have been warmed-up for five to ten minutes. The warm-up is low key. Relaxed walking, jogging and stopping gradually bring the young horse to the beginning of intensive training. The warm-down reverses the process. Both of these periods, done correctly, do not reduce the attention span. The young stock horse may have been ridden thirty minutes to an hour, but the pressure to perform was limited to fifteen to twenty minutes.

As with all facets of training, timing and feel are the keys which separate the tinhorns from the old timers . . . The words, "quit on a good note," reflect years of experience with these aspects.

As you approach the upper limit of your horse's attention span, look for a stopping point. If no recognition is given to the horse's attention span, a trainer often will have preconceived expectations for the animal's progress. The trainer may refuse to stop working on a particular maneuver until it is accomplished. This attitude can lead to a dead end. As the colt overloads, he no longer desires to achieve or try. Unable to accomplish his goal, the trainer becomes frustrated with the horse, and the horse becomes increasingly resistant to training. Enter the battle of wills. Exit the opportunity for positive training. Even if the trainer wins the round and convinces the horse to perform the task, the war has been lost. The horse has been taught to dislike training. Refractory behavior most certainly has been paired with this maneuver.

When looking for that good note on which to quit, use a sliding scale that measures progress. If the horse has not been overly taxed physically or mentally, you can expect him to make a strong effort to perform correctly so he can be rewarded and rested (stopped). On the other hand, if the horse is nearing the end of his rope, you should realize the immediate need to terminate the session. Quit after almost any change that could be considered a step in the right direction.

As with all facets of training, timing and feel are the keys which separate the tinhorns from old timers like Pig Hall. The words, "quit on a good note," reflect years of experience which honed the timing to know when to quit and sharpened the feel to sense when the horse's effort is enough. This simple phrase holds one of the sacred commandments of training. Reach for understanding and it will, undoubtedly, make you a better trainer.

10

A LITTLE IS GOOD,
A LOT IS NOT

 Somewhere in the southwestern United States, a lone bronc-stomper runs his rope around an 8-inch snubbing post of a 60-foot circular pen. The dust rising into the still hot air attests to the bronc's protest when he was choked and his head drawn up tight against the post. The date is 1885.

At this point, the old cowboy slips a braided hackamore over the horse's head. He begins to sack out the colt by flipping an old blanket over the horse's shoulders and back. If the bronc is worth his salt, dust and dirt will fly some more until it turns to mud as it mixes with the sweat pouring off both bodies.

The fit begins to die down as the mustang's survival instincts kick in. With the horse's head tied securely to the post, the horse wrangler, carrying the saddle, approaches him at the shoulder.

The bronc fails to submit. With the only part of body still free to resist, the bronc fires a couple of well aimed blows with his hind legs. Placing the saddle back down on the ground, the seasoned bronc-stomper pulls out a scarf and another rope. The colt has left the old timer no choice but to tie up a hind foot and blindfold the cunning critter.

The blindfold is twisted into the cheekpiece on either side of the hackamore and slowly slid over the bronc's eyes. Next the old braided rope is looped around the neck and tied with a bowline knot, leaving about 16 feet of line free to snare a back leg. Another struggle takes place before the rope can be drawn back through the neck loop and tied off.

Next the saddle goes on and the cinch is pulled up tight. A lot of fight has gone out of this previously unrestrained animal. The bronc-stomper, after unhooking the tie to the post, now earns his name and his pay. He slithers up into the saddle with the stealth of a rattlesnake stalking a rat and drops lightly into the depth of the horse's back. He reaches down easy to loosen the blindfold, then unties the slip knot holding the hind foot off the ground.

The horse, apparently blinded by the bright overhead sun, stands quietly. The rider tickles his sides with a light rake of the spurs — Explosion! It is man's athletic ability against that of the horse. The spurs rake, the quirt whips the flanks of the sweat soaked horse. In a few minutes the horse gives up and runs, then tires to a jog. The day's lesson is over.

The fight or flight syndrome is still built into most horses born in the twenty-first century. The bucking, stomping, and squalling is the horse's reaction to a simulated predator attack.

This method for breaking horses has been around a long time and is probably responsible for the old horsemen's saying: "There never was a horse who couldn't be rode and there never was a cowboy that couldn't be throwed." The truth in these words is founded upon an instinctive fear of horses. Horses fear being pounced on by creatures that land on their backs. Peaceful grazing animals are eaten by predators who behave like this. Four thousand years of domestication has not erased this survival instinct. The fight or flight syndrome is still built into most horses born in the twenty-first century. The bucking, stomping, and squalling is the horse's reaction to a simulated predator attack.

Unfortunately, this innate fear is not the only one which plagues horses. Specific horses may be afraid of sudden movements, loud noises, cars, trains, sonic booms, or being bound around the heart-girth. The list goes on, leaving the horse trainer to figure the best way to handle these fears.

Historically there have been two major approaches. The one most folks think of first is the one described in the opening story — flooding. It works well on many horses, but it runs a high risk of both physical and mental injury. This technique starts by identifying what is frightening the horse. Then the frightening stimulus is applied full strength while preventing the horse from escaping it. The frightening stimulus is kept up until the horse either dies or gets used to it.

While effective on some horses, the thrashing and fighting of a terrified horse can create physical damage to the barn, the horse and the human. The mental damage suffered by many horses is often just as bad, although more subtle. They do what we want, but in a mechanical sort of way without any willingness. Some weaker horses snap mentally and are never quite right afterwards. Their spirit is completely broken.

There are also some problems if the flooding is not completed. For instance, when trainers broke horses with the flooding technique used by the old bronc-stomper, it was important for the rider to stay in the saddle until the horse stopped showing fear. If the horse managed to throw the bronc rider, flooding was not completed. Instead the horse learned that fighting could eliminate the cause of his fears. Therefore many trainers today use flooding only as a last resort, when all else has failed. They also keep in mind that if you are going to flood, you had better do it properly.

The other approach is slower and requires more patience, but is much safer since it runs a very low risk of physical or mental injury. It is called progressive desensitization by some and systematic desensitization by others. We will simply call it desensitization. As with flooding, desensitizing begins by identifying the horse's fear. Once identified, the trainer decreases the object of the horse's fear to a level that no longer bothers the horse. Next the frightening stimulus is presented to the horse at this no fear level. In very small increments the intensity of the stimulus is increased, as long as the horse remains 100 percent calm. If at any time, the horse shows signs of fear it indicates the trainer has advanced too quickly. The solution is to fall back to a level that the horse can handle, and continue the process from there.

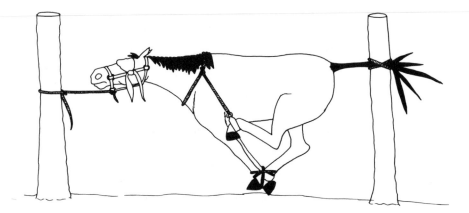

Desensitizing takes more time, but the benefits are substantial. The horse does not need to thrash and fight to escape. Consequently there is far less chance of physical damage to the barn, the horse or the human. Mentally, horses find this method less stressful, which preserves the spirit so prized by good horsemen.

A good example of desensitizing a horse's fear of carrying a rider is the method we call "breaking without force" or "tackless training." Pressure on the horse's back is applied at a level the horse will accept without fear. This can be merely a hand placed on his back. The next step would be two hands. When the horse feels comfortable with that, an arm or two may be pressed across his back. By continuing with such small steps, and never going to the next step until the horse is comfortable, you will soon be bellied across his back. Sitting up is only one more small step. The horse has been desensitized to carrying a human without the thrashing, fighting and damage so characteristic of the flooding approach.

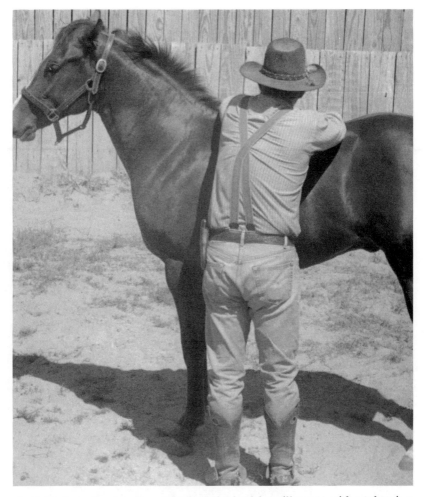

Applying pressure on a horse's back at the level he will accept without fear is a good example of a desensitization technique.

Spooky horses are usually trained best using desensitization training. Flooding can destroy these sensitive animals. Whatever stimulus causes them to spook can be decreased and reintroduced at a level they can accept. By gradually increasing exposure to the fear object these horses will learn to ignore what previously frightened them. For example, horses with fears of loud noises, such as thunder, can be desensitized using high quality tape recordings. The volume can be turned down to an acceptable level, then gradually raised in stages. One major advantage of tape recordings is that it allows you to present the fear at opportune moments such as feeding time.

A horse that strongly objects to carrying a sack of rattling cans is a more common problem for trail riders. The wildest beast easily can be desensitized by using this simple technique: start by quietly shaking a sack of cans at a distance from the horse where he shows interest but not fear. Slowly increase the sound to its loudest. Step in closer and repeat the sequence. If the horse should show fear at any point decrease the noise level, step back or stop the sound completely. Walk up to the horse with the sack and let him investigate. Once his curiosity is satisfied, return to an acceptable location and begin desensitization again. It won't be long until the horse will show no apprehension about what was once the "horse eating sack."

Desensitizing also works well on young horses because they aren't mature enough to handle a great deal of stress. A young horse has to learn to accept a myriad of new experiences. One difficult lesson is the horse's acceptance of restraint. Tying a weanling up hard and fast, either to a wall or a snubbing post, is an example of flooding. The pressure is relentless and inescapable. He must submit or die. A few die. Some break legs, or pull down their heads — slipping the Atlas vertebrae which results in a permanent canted head position.

A less traumatic approach to teaching restraint exists using desensitization techniques. By haltering a young foal and leading him along with his dam, the foal learns restraint in increments. At first the foal will try to follow his dam's lead. The new situation, the halter, will inevitably cause him to pull away. Small amounts of pressure will bring him under control because he wants to return to his dam. Increasing the time before the foal can return to his mother's side establishes gradual control without unnecessary fear.

As you can see, desensitization is a very simple concept. To change concepts to useful tools for training horses requires an understanding of the horse. You must be always willing to let the horse tell you how much he can take and when he has had enough. Without the ability or desire to read a horse, concepts will always be concepts. A union of horse and human will never exist.

By haltering a young foal and leading him along with his dam, the foal learns restraint in increments.

11
CONSISTENCY

Consistent rules with consistent consequences for failure to comply are the basis for developing a relationship with a horse. This concept is easy to accomplish because the natural behavior of horses is governed by strict and unyielding rules of protocol. In the herd, the submissive must show respect to the dominant. The young must not invade the personal space of the elders. Higher ranking members of the herd are not to be ignored. Herd laws are consistent within all equine herds, only the individuals are different. This consistency gives the horse a sense of harmony. He knows how he fits into his world.

Today's horse must learn a dependence upon man. For the horse to be comfortable in this arrangement, the alliance must be structured so that the horse understands his role and knows what behavior is considered proper. Rules which make most sense to horses are ones that are consistent with herd life. The rules for breeding stallions listed above are based on normal breeding conduct. Although it may take a fight to convince the stallion to do it right, learning will be easier because the rules are the same as a mare would teach him in the wild.

Controlling a 1,200-pound breeding stallion with a few pieces of leather and a chain demands rules of behavior that are chiseled in stone:

1. The stallion should approach the mare by walking beside, but not in front of the shoulder of the horseman.

2. The stallion should never take slack out of the leadline.

3. The stallion always should have at least one eye and ear paying attention to his handler.

4. The stallion should approach the mare's head from the side and talk nicely to her.

5. Upon command, he should back up and approach the mare at the shoulder where he may tease.

6. Upon command, the horse should back up and approach the mare at the hip. Teasing may again proceed.

7. Upon command, the stallion should back up and await a signal to mount the mare.

8. At no time shall the stallion be allowed to savage a mare.

9. After breeding, the stallion should be expected to stand quietly around the mare's tail for a few minutes.

These rules are very black and white. Attempts to deviate are always dealt with swiftly.

In a herd, the submissive must show respect to the dominant.

It is the same for all horses. The rules of basic behavior must be set forth and consistently upheld. What you will and won't allow should be equally clear to both you and the horse.

Wishy-washy behavior from a dominant herd member is not allowed. In our herd of two, man must be the dominant member. Therefore, you have to make and uphold the law. To keep this from being a monumental task, don't make rules you are not going to always enforce. Think long and hard before you add a law to your list.

In a herd of two, man must be the dominant member.

Besides the basic commandments about kicking, biting, or otherwise mauling, most other important rules deal with gaining and maintaining a horse's respect. Respect is probably the single most important factor in harmonious living with an animal which outweighs us by close to 1,000 pounds. Without respect we are likely to be run over, kicked at, jumped on or otherwise be pushed around. This becomes a major concern when dealing with horses in groups.

The roughest time to deal with a horse herd is at feeding time. Entering a field of ten to fifteen horses while carrying feed buckets can be as dangerous as being sent to the front line. Crowding around you, the horses begin to bicker about who should get the first nibble. Some dive at each other while others let hoofs fly. Thousand-pound bodies dart this way and that to escape blows.

As you walk through a herd, always project enough authority to move horses out of your way.

To avoid this situation you must order the herd to a more natural social system. As you enter the paddock protect your personal space as though you were a dominant member of the herd. Do not allow any horse to approach closer than ten feet. As you walk through the herd always project enough authority to force the animals out of your way. You should never make submissive gestures such as walking around one of the horses. Never let one of the more submissive horses follow behind you. Only the most dominant individual should be allowed at the outer limits of your protected territory. All horses should stay away from the feeding station until you leave.

To put this into practice initially, it may be necessary to threaten the horses aggressively or carry a big stick. Once established you can never let your projected authority be questioned. All attempts should be met with a swift and consistent reprisal. Once this system becomes routine, a natural order will be established in a man-made environment.

Consistency also plays an important role in training. Consistency allows a horse to figure out what is being asked. Its antithesis, inconsistency, drives a horse into frustration, and God forbid, learned helplessness. Young trainers often forget this important principle as they get discouraged when failing to teach a horse a new manuever. The old saying, "There are many ways to skin a cat," becomes their downfall rather than their redeeming grace. The scenario seems to go like this:

Armed with a few tried and true methods, a young trainer begins with his favorite. For a reason unbeknownst to him, his preferred choice fails to get the desired results in the normal length of time. Insecure in his ability, the neophyte trainer decides to try another technique. The confused horse begins to get frustrated. The young trainer begins to lose his patience and anger builds. He changes to yet another system.

This completely boggles the green colt's mind. The trainer, in his state of frustration, pounds on the colt. Punishment becomes the reward for every wrong response. The horse becomes fractious; learning ceases. The whole training session falls apart and it is the fault of the young trainer.

Rules which make most sense to horses are ones that are consistant with herd life. The rules for breeding stallions are based on normal breeding conduct.

Where did it go wrong? It probably began with the training technique selected for this horse. One reason there are so many ways to teach horses any given maneuver is because they don't all work equally well on every horse. Experienced horsemen know which technique has the best odds of working on a specific horse. Once they make the decision, they ride the system through to the end.

This doesn't mean that they can't be wrong. Even the best suited system needs to be adapted to fit each horse individually. The

63

minor variations, however, do not affect the overall consistent presentation of the technique. Let's see how this works.

The cue for turning that I have found easiest for most horses to understand is based upon their natural response to body balance points and pressure. To ask a horse to turn right at a walk, I begin by shifting my weight slightly onto the right hip. The horse's natural response to this imbalance is to move his body to the right to get back under the weight. This sets the green colt's mind in the right direction. Next, (and by next, I mean in the next tenth of a second), I twist my upper body to the right with exactly the amount of turn that I wish the colt to make. The sharper the turn the more forward balance must be added to the side twist. Finally some directional impulsion is added by a tap of the outside leg (in this case, the left leg).

A very light, sensitive horse will read this cue and turn to the right. Nonattentive naive horses or those who are not so light need some minor variations, but the cue always begins in the same way. First shift the seat and upper body and then bring in the leg. There is never any variation in the body cue for the specific turn.

Modifications begin with the leg cue. The tap may become a bump, a thud, a bang, or the leg may be used in different positions around the hearthgirth. The purpose of variations is to find a way to communicate what is being asked. As a last resort, I will go to the reins, first using light pressure to the right. Then I modify the technique, searching for the exact variation that fits the individual horse.

Successful training starts with clear decisions about your relationship with horses and the goals you wish to achieve. Being consistent, which is oftentimes mistaken for being stubborn, bullheaded or hardheaded, is at least half the battle in getting results.

12

ELIMINATING UNDESIRABLE BEHAVIOR

 Horses are not born bad actors. They are made. It may seem adorable to have a foal nip at you but it is never fun when that horse grows up biting. Encouraging foals to rear up and playfully paw and strike at you is not my idea of an enjoyable diversion. It is only a matter of time until someone is going to knock the dickens out of them for playing. Foals must learn to relate to people in a respectable way. The behavior patterns built during the first few years can last a lifetime.

Early training also takes its toll in producing undesirable behaviors. Horses are driven, pushed, coerced or abused into undesirable behaviors by trainers who lack feeling about a horse's individuality. Whatever the cause, once the unacceptable behavior appears it must be dealt with. There are three fundamental approaches to curing dangerous behavior: ignore the behavior; train an incompatible behavior; or administer punishment. Each method has advantages and disadvantages. They will not all work equally well under the same circumstance. In fact, when I was younger I wasn't even sure that ignoring the behavior was a viable alternative. I figured that if an animal did something I thought was bad, I needed to deliver a good whack to tell him not to behave that way again or else. The first light shed upon how this technique actually might be useful happened one afternoon as I was helping an Indian move some Angus heifers down a lane on foot.

As soon as the heifers gained momentum in the chute, we started to crowd them. Pow! One heifer had taken dead aim and kicked the Indian in the shinbone. The hit sounded like a small bore rifle shot. I turned to look, expecting to see him grimacing in pain and cussing that cow. I was astonished to see that his facial expression had not changed. Nor was there any hitch in his stride. I thought to myself that Indian must have a wooden leg and he just never told anyone about it.

In a few minutes we closed the pen gate. Not wanting to pry into matters which didn't concern me, I asked casually, "Didn't that cow kick you pretty hard back there?"

"Yep," he says without any more response.

"Well, didn't it hurt?" I was giving up on seeming only mildly interested.

"Yep, it hurt," came the reply, but still no further explanation.

"How come, then, you didn't do or say something," I asked, figuring that maybe I would find out about the wooden leg.

He answered, "If I had, then the cow would have known she hurt me." I was confused, but not wanting to appear ignorant, I dropped the subject.

It finally dawned on me that this incident was an example of eliminating an undesirable behavior by not rewarding it.

Several times over the next few years I thought about this incidence and what the implications might be. It finally dawned on me that this incident was an example of eliminating an undesirable behavior by not rewarding it. The cow kicked the human because he was doing something she didn't like. If the Indian had reacted in the expected manner the heifer would have known the kick did what it was supposed to do. She then would have been more likely to try it again the next time a human invoked her displeasure. Since the kick solicited no response the cow was probably as confused as I was. If her kicking behavior was repeated a few more times without response, it is likely the heifer would feel she was wasting her energy and give up the practice.

Since most folks are not as stoic as this particular Indian, the key to using this training technique is to decide which behaviors can be extinguished by lack of human response. One such behavior might be the pawing and stomping of an impatient horse. If a behavior gets no response it will usually go away. Several years ago I got the opportunity to try this technique when I went into a stall to catch a rather roguish stallion.

I wasn't in the stall door more than a step or two when the stallion wheeled and grabbed my arm with his teeth. I was caught. As the stallion clinched his teeth on my forearm, I had a flashback to the kicking cow incident. I decided to pretend that I didn't feel a thing.

The stallion, for a moment, seemed surprised. As the initial confusion passed, the horse seemed to get madder. I guess he decided he wasn't biting hard enough because he began to really lock down on my arm and shake his head. Unable to stand it any longer, I stuck the thumb of my free arm in his eye. Thank God he turned loose! The stud ran to the back of the stall, cowered in the corner and looked at me like he was eyeing a ghost. As I walked up to him he was quivering. I snapped the leadshank on and lead him out of the stall. As he sidepassed down the hall, his eyes bugged out as if he was watching the Great Spirit who had temporarily taken on a human form.

As you can see, rogues do not always respond to this passive method of eliminating bad behaviors, but it did surprise the stallion long enough to give me an edge. Beware of using this approach on demented horses. Because their behavior makes little sense to themselves, it is difficult to manipulate them using standard techniques. Leave the crazy ones to those who are crazy enough to fool with them.

Rearing is a more common vice found in riding horses. The standard response is to try to eliminate the problem by using some form of punishment. Unfortunately, bashing a horse over the head with a stick does not always work. In the first place, some horses have a difficult time associating the lick on the head to rearing.

67

This makes the punishment meaningless. Secondly, even if the horse does make the connection between the hit and the rearing his response may be to go higher to avoid the punishment. In fact, the horse may learn that if he flips over completely, the rider will not have time to bash at all. At best, hitting a horse over the head will lead to head shyness. Every time the horse catches a glimpse of movement from above he will dodge to escape the hits he expects.

I believe this situation lends itself best to training incompatible behavior. Although rearing can develop into a life threatening dilemma, it begins in stages.

For example, a trainer may use a lot of pressure and restraint. Consequently, the horse becomes frustrated and begins to look for a way to escape or vent his energy. The horse can not go forward without more pressure applied to his head and mouth. He can not go backward or sideways without being driven by the heels of the rider. The horse feels he is in a vice. The only choices left are to lie down or rear up.

There are several ways to eliminate this situation. The horse can be relaxed, the pressure and restraint removed, and the situation analyzed to figure out the problem. But to continue with our example, let's follow our novice trainer.

The first attempt at rearing is just a few inches off the ground. The rider, taken by surprise is intimidated and releases the pressure. Rearing has now been rewarded. But the next time the horse rears a few inches, his rider is ready. So the horse rears higher in order to be rewarded. The process is repeated, until, by successive approximation, the horse learns exactly how high to rear to intimidate his rider enough to gain control.

Once this happens, breaking the habit can be difficult. However, somewhere between the first low rear and the higher dangerous rear, an incompatible move can be taught. When a horse raises up he is very susceptible to be pulled off balance. Snatching him to the side before he has totally committed to the rear will force him to either fall sideways or return to the ground. This also replaces backward pressure with side pressure which will prevent him from charging forward. Once on the ground, the trainer should continue to circle the horse until he is able to vent the hostile energy. In no time, the rear can be changed into a spin — a much safer move to ride. We have now traded a dangerous and intimidating behavior, (rearing or flipping), that cannot be tolerated, for one (spinning), that the trainer can endure long enough to correct the original problem.

Punishment causes refractory behavior towards learning. Therefore, I believe using punishment as a teaching tool should be the last choice.

Training an incompatible behavior presents the opportunity to turn a bad situation into a positive learning experience without the negative side effects associated with punishment. Punishment causes refractory behavior towards learning. Therefore, I believe using punishment as a teaching tool should be the last choice.

Several years ago I watched with great interest a young man from Alvin, Texas, train a calf-roping horse. The horse was a rather high-headed, fractious bay gelding of uncertain ancestry who had proven fairly difficult to train for this event.

To speed the training process along the young horseman had developed a rather crude but effective technique to get the horse to stop and work the rope. He had a large spring-loaded rat trap, the kind which releases a loop of wire around the rat's neck when the cheese is lifted. He had modified the trap by sawing off the half of the board where the wire loop was designed to hit. The remaining half was then tied into the brow band of the horse's bridle. If the trigger was sprung, the wire loop would smack the horse on the forehead.

The trigger was redesigned by running a string from the cheese holder to a weight. When the weight was placed in the stirrup the trap was set.

When the young rider roped a calf, he would holler whoa as he jumped down to tie the calf. As his boot left the stirrup, it would cause the weight to drop, setting off the trap. The wire loop would plant right between the horse's eyes, reminding him to stop and back up.

The first time this machinery was applied to this high-headed, high-spirited animal, it did the job. The horse backed up real fast. I guess since it worked so well, the young roper decided to use it every time. It only took a few times for the horse to learn that no matter how hard he stopped and ran back, he still got whacked in the head.

Soon he refused to go into the roping box. The horse had learned that chasing calves was a painful thing to do and he was going to try his best not to do it. The only way to get him in was to have one person lead him while another whipped him from behind.

Forced to participate, he knew he could not escape the pain if he stopped. As soon as the rope fell around the calf's neck the horse ran wild, refusing to stop no matter how hard his rider pulled on the reins. He wasn't about to let this guy get off. This created trouble for the calf tied hard and fast to a runaway horse. As the horse ran past the calf, the whiplash was strong enough to throw the horse off stride. The horse slipped down, throwing his rider to the ground and releasing the rat trap. When the trap popped, the horse got up and ran backwards over top of the roper.

The calf, still tied to the horn, began to run in circles, wrapping the roper and his horse into a well-tied bundle. Now, no one likes being wound up in a rope, but it's particularly uncomfortable when you're wound up with a 1,200-pound half-crazed horse and a terrified 300-pound calf. What a wreck!

All punishment training does not end in quite as dramatic a scene as this example, but the point remains the same. There are serious side effects from using punishment as the primary training tool. It should be avoided whenever possible.

13
LIMITED DISTRACTIONS

 Will a horse train faster if distractions are eliminated or minimized? The answer to this question is yes. But, what happens to the horse trained in isolation when he goes on a trail ride or to a horse show ? What happens when a covey of quail flush from underneath the colt's nose? Or when a Mack truck hits his air horn? Usually disaster!

If learning can be hurried by training with minimum distractions, is there a way to increase trainability while avoiding later perplexing stimuli? How much distraction is ideal to maximize trainability? To answer some of these questions six halter-broken yearlings who had been turned out since weaning were brought in for prebreaking ground work. Lounge training would include walk, trot, canter, stop, and reverse. Three of the animals would receive their lessons in a pen surrounded by several highrise buildings adjoining a busy road. The other three would be trained in a soundproof, completely closed quonset hut. Each horse was worked fifteen minutes a day. After four days the horses in the soundproof quonset hut were two days ahead of the other group.

The next step was to bring the three which had been trained with limited distraction into a world where they would be bombarded by sights and sounds unrelated to training. The result was an immediate regression in performance. They had to learn to pay attention to the trainer's cues in spite of the distractions. These three, however, were still ahead of the three which were trained with the distractions present all along.

In the previous example, the results suggests that it is better to first train the horse in isolation and introduce distractions later. In this way we are dividing the problem rather than forcing the horse to handle too many stimuli at one time.

Unfortunately, most of us don't have a soundproof booth big enough in which to ride. So how do we go about using this training information in an everyday situation? For years, seasoned horse trainers have worked around the problem by working green colts when activity around the training facility is minimal. For example, many trainers ride early in the morning or late at night.

The more training done on a youngster without having to beat and bang on him for his attention, the quicker the learning will be. Suppose you are breaking a young filly that is a bit spooky. Everything seems to distract her. She jumps at every noise and runs from the falling leaves. In order to make this filly a useful horse you have got to get her trust. Imagine trying to step up on her during five o'clock rush hour. The commotion is too much for this young fractious filly. You are forced to beat her to get her attention. The force adds to the distraction. The filly becomes frantic. The circle begins. She gets higher. You have to use more pressure to get her attention. This is a very long road to developing trust between horse and human.

Will a horse train faster if distractions are eliminated or minimized? The answer to this question is yes.

On the other hand, let's imagine we handled this filly with a little more finesse. By having just a little insight into her disposition and mental abilities, we could positively manipulate this filly's first training session.

The filly must be familiar and comfortable in the breaking pen. Turn her into the training area so she can become familiar with the sounds, smells, and shadows. This will reduce her fear and lessen the stimuli which will distract her learning.

72

Choose the quietest time of day for her lesson. Patiently show her what is expected. From the beginning the filly must look to you for support. If she gets spooked you must make her feel secure. Nothing will be able to get her when she is under the control of her benevolent human companion. With each subsequent training situation, it is inevitable that this budding relationship will be tested. Within a few days, the first reaction of this fractious young filly to unexpected distractions should be to look to you for guidance.

Limited distractions during initial training helps all horses develop a base before having to cope with the outside world. Even the most calm, cool and collected horse cannot be expected to walk out of the arena and onto the trail for the first time without a considerable reduction in his level of training. A horse with any mind at all will show interest in new sights and smells. You may think that your horse has forgotten all training. This is not the case at all. He is not giving you all his attention because he is being bombarded with new stimuli.

To help the youngster through this stage, send the green colt out with a seasoned horse. Let the older horse lead the way, giving the colt a steady horse model. Riding the green colt takes a special kind of attitude. Do not expect him to be responsive at first. Let him follow along. He will wander over here and over there. He will get behind and want to trot to catch up. Let him. Let him explore his environment for the very first time with a rider on his back. Soon the colt will be able to handle the new situation and give some attention to you. When you feel him ask for direction, give it. By the end of an hour ride, the youngster should be back in your hands. You now have two training environments: the pen and the trail. Each day as you increase his performance level in the pen your colt will show more attention on the trail.

For many trainers, the trail is a relaxing way to end a hard training session. Now distractions aid training. They allow the young horse to unwind from the pressure of performance. With his trainer expecting less perfection, the youngster is gradually warmed down and released into his non-human environment.

Send a green colt out with a seasoned horse.

14
THE NICE
HORSY SYNDROME

 Pets do not make performance horses. I have made that statement probably a thousand times over the past twenty- five years. The response I invariably get is: "Why not? I like my horse and I want my horse to like me."

Obviously we all like horses or we wouldn't be messing with them. Horses, on the other hand, do not build relationships on like but rather on respect.

Pet horses are rewarded for being companions for their owners. They are petted, rubbed and loved for just being there. Carrots, sugar and other candies are given for the pure joy of giving by the owner. Should the pet behave in a naughty manner, discipline is usually limited to a minor scolding. Hitting him may make him not like you. Also, the pet horse is not asked to do too much. In fact, the horse usually decides how much to give and his owner is usually pleased. Our pet horse will rub against us without invitation. Being a companion animal, our pet horse takes it for granted that he can move freely around us without worrying if he is behaving properly.

Let's now look at this situation through the horse's eyes. Remember he bases relationships on herding rules. In the herd, affiliations are based on respect. Horses respect those higher in the pecking order and do not respect those below.

Essentially, a higher ranking horse will control lower ranking horses. He will walk freely into their personal space and expect them to move. He will bump them, threaten them and expect no more than an irritated, (but not aggressive) response.

There is similarity in the relationships between the pet horse and his owner, and the dominant horse and the submissive. These similarities also are obvious to the horse. A pet horse usually sees himself as the dominant, or equal, member of the herd of man and horse. This creates problems in training.

In the herd, lower ranking members of the herd do not control, influence or otherwise train higher ranking horses. You are going to have a difficult time training your horse since he perceives you as the submissive member of the partnership.

I know that most pet horse owners do not believe themselves to be subservient. But many will admit that they feel like their companions are their equals. Often they offer their horse the opportunity to decide about the day's activities. Do you feel like a brisk gallop? Do you feel up to jumping a six-foot fence? The answer may be no because the alternative is more appealing. Do you feel like practicing lead changes from a canter or would you rather eat grass with the other horses?

These may be the kind of choices you would offer your best friend. They are not the kind of choices you offer to someone you wish to influence. You wouldn't ask a child whether he would like to clean up his room or go play a new game. Rooms would never get cleaned using that approach. Your only hope of getting any training done using this technique would be to phrase a question like: "Do you want to bring in the groceries or put them away?" Both responses are at least, advantageous to the partner who is trying to control the situation. Training might occur.

These problems are minor compared to the one created when the positive reinforcer, praise, is depreciated. Like the law of supply and demand, the more plentiful and available an object, the less value it has. If a horse can get praise, attention, petting, rubbing and other affirmative gestures without performing, then why should he exert himself for that particular reward. Once we lose this powerful reinforcer, we have nothing to replace it with. Punishment is the only training tool left.

I cringe when an owner unloads a horse to be trained and tells me I won't have any trouble with the horse. The owner says the horse is a perfect angel, does everything he asks and has never made a wrong move in her whole life. Chances are she has never been asked to make any move in her whole life. In fact she has probably never been asked to do anything. Invariably, as I take the nice horse's leadshank she tries to run over the top of me. I bury my instincts to put the filly in line. (The owners would never understand.) A subtle but well-timed yank gets a momentarily startled look from the spoiled horse. It lasts long enough to herd the young horse into the stall without getting jumped or stepped on.

I hate training these kind of horses because I hate what it takes to bring their world back in order. In my barn, man is the dominant member of the herd. To gain this position I will have to fight this filly for dominance just like another horse would.

Owners ultimately force horses to undergo this attitude adjustment. They never think about the horse's transition from a spoiled horse to a performance horse. If they did, they would be sure not to make pets of their horses.

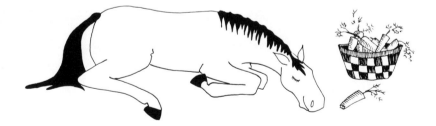